THE CTS
COMPANION TO READING
THE NEW TESTAMENT

by
Fr Adrian Graffy

*All booklets are published thanks to the
generous support of the members of the
Catholic Truth Society*

CATHOLIC TRUTH SOCIETY
PUBLISHERS TO THE HOLY SEE

2

CONTENTS

THE BOOKS OF THE NEW TESTAMENT

The Gospels *3 Synoptic Gospels* Matthew Mark Luke *and* John	Philippians Colossians I & II Thessalonians I & II Timothy Titus Philemon
	Hebrews
Acts of the Apostles	***Catholic Epistles*** James I & II Peter I, II & III John Jude
The Pauline Letters Romans I & II Corinthians Galatians Ephesians	Revelation of John (or Apocalypse)

INTRODUCTION

God speaks through the Son

"At various times in the past, and in various different ways, God spoke to our ancestors through the prophets. Now, in these last days, God has spoken to us through the Son." *(Hebrews 1:1-2)*

Christianity, in common with Judaism, proclaims belief in a God who reaches out to people, a God who communicates, a God who reveals. For Christians the climax of God's reaching out, God's communication, God's revelation, comes in Jesus, the Son of God. In the CTS Companion to Reading the Old Testament *(Sc 69)*we explored how God spoke to our ancestors through the inspired writers of the Old Testament. This booklet sets out to explore how God spoke to us through the Son. The document of the Second Vatican Council on the Bible, known as the "Dogmatic Constitution on Divine Revelation", usually referred to with its first two Latin words *Dei Verbum* ("Word of God"), proclaims the faith of Christians that the fulness of God's revelation is to be found in Jesus Christ *(Dei Verbum n.2)*.

The Church declares that God reaches out to human beings through the Word. God condescends to speak to human beings at first through the inspired writers of the Old Testament. God's Word is expressed in human language, for otherwise our limited human minds could not grasp it. At the appointed time God speaks through the Son, who takes on our human condition so that human beings can relate to and believe in the Son of God. The writers of the New Testament tell us that this Son of God is the Word of God, for the Son in becoming man reveals God to us and invites us to respond and to receive new life. The First Letter of John declares: "What was from the beginning, what we have heard, what we have seen with our eyes, what we have watched and what our hands have touched, the Word of life is what we proclaim." *(1 John 1:1)* The Son of God who was always with God became a human being so that in him God could reach out, communicate and reveal the way to life.

Reading and Praying the New Testament

The purpose of this short introduction is not simply to impart information about the New Testament. In order to be nourished by the Scriptures we need to approach them in a spirit of peace and prayerfulness. But information about them will assist us to understand and derive more from our reading. The Church's ancient practice of *lectio divina* (or "divine reading") has been taken up by many people in recent times. At its simplest, it is the practice of reading the Scriptures in a prayerful and meditative way.

Lectio divina can also be practised in groups. This booklet can be used to provide background for anyone wishing to engage in the prayerful reading of any of the books of the New Testament.

It is also possible to use this booklet to accompany the cycle of readings at Sunday Mass or at Masses in the week. The Gospels of Matthew, Mark and Luke are read on the Sundays of successive years, while the Gospel of John is reserved for particular Sundays of Lent and Easter. The weekday Lectionary in Ordinary Time takes us through the Gospels of Mark, Matthew and Luke, in that order. Once again the Gospel of John is read on certain weekdays in Lent and Easter. All the other books of the New Testament also receive their allotted time. While some parts of the Old Testament never appear in the Lectionary, all books of the New Testament are read. It is therefore quite possible to cover the New Testament by accompanying the Sunday and weekday Lectionary with meditative reading of the New Testament. At times in the weekday Lectionary, of course, the first reading will be taken not from the New Testament but from the Old Testament.

Which Bible should I read?

A question people often ask when deciding to read the Bible more regularly is "which Bible should I read?" A rich and somewhat bewildering variety of translations and editions of the Bible can be found in religious bookshops these days. To aid understanding it is clearly best to choose a modern translation. The "King James Bible", also known as the "Authorised Version", contains some of the most beautiful English ever written and is rightly treasured as a work of literature. It is, however, not easy for modern readers to understand, and, being written in the early 17th century, lacks the benefit of later progress in understanding the Scriptures. Catholic translations like the "Douai Bible" and the "Knox Bible" are also dated, and these Bibles also suffer from the fact that they were translated not from the original languages but from the Latin Vulgate translation, the official Latin translation used by the church since the fifth century.

To assist understanding the Catholic Church encourages the production of annotated Bibles. The annotated "Jerusalem Bible" or its successor the "New Jerusalem Bible" not only provide useful information in the notes whether you read the study edition or the reader's edition, but also neatly divide the text into manageable sections rather than presenting it without breaks. Each section is given a title so that the reader is assisted in grasping the meaning. The annotated "Revised Standard Version" and "New Revised Standard Version" have similar strengths. These are the Bibles which would be best suited to Catholic readers today. Several different editions of each translation are often available. Examine them and choose the Bible which seems most attractive.

Mention should also be made of the "New International Version", a widely-available Bible which reflects more conservative positions on interpretation. The "New English Bible" and its successor the "Revised English Bible" provide translations in modern English style and take less conservative positions. The "Good News Bible" seems a very attractive translation, but it often paraphrases a translation to make the text more intelligible and will not be the best version for anyone wanting to get close to the original expressions of the biblical writers. Whatever Bible you buy, it is most important to make sure that it contains the "deutero-canonical" books which are described as "the apocrypha" in non-Catholic Bibles.

The Books of the New Testament

The New Testament contains the record of the life, death and resurrection of Jesus, the Son of God. It also begins to explore how disciples of Jesus are to live in the world amid changing circumstances. The most well-known and cherished parts of the New Testament are the four books we know as gospels. Their ancient titles attribute them to Matthew, Mark, Luke and John. In the original Greek a gospel is called *euaggelion*, which means "good news". The English word "gospel" is appropriately derived from the ancient English for "good news". The climax of these gospels comes in the death and resurrection of Jesus. It is those events which are also the focus of the good news preached by the apostles and disciples. This is seen clearly in the Letters of St Paul and in the sermons in the Acts of the Apostles. The four gospels were accepted as authoritative, or "canonical", by the Church because they were seen to provide true witness to the life of Jesus and because they proclaimed the faith of Christians about Jesus: that he was the Son of God, and that he died and was raised by the Father to open the way to life for God's people.

The book called the "Acts of the Apostles" is unique in the New Testament, because it takes the story beyond the appearances of the risen Jesus to provide an account of the life of the early Church.

The second major group of books is the collection of the letters of the apostle Paul. The letters give advice on issues arising in the lives of the various Christian communities, and doctrine concerning Jesus and his role in God's plan for human beings is elaborated. Some of the letters in this "Pauline corpus", particularly those to Timothy and Titus, are considered by many to have been compiled by disciples of Paul. Everyone agrees that the Letter to the Hebrews was not written by Paul.

There are other letters too in the New Testament. Three letters are attributed to St John, and the so-called "catholic" epistles, given this name because they have no specific destination, are attributed to Peter, James and Jude.

The final and most challenging book of the New Testament is known as the Book of Revelation, or the Apocalypse. Its extraordinary visions direct the gaze of Christians towards the unimaginable life of the world to come.

THE GOSPELS

The nature of a gospel

To understand the nature of the writings we call gospels
we could do no better than refer to *Dei Verbum*, the document on Divine Revelation of the Second Vatican
Council. This is the authoritative teaching of the Catholic
Church on the Bible. In Chapter 5 of this document it is
clearly stated that the gospels came about as a result of a
process of development. Jesus made an extraordinary
impact on the people of his day, by his teaching and healing, but above all by his death and resurrection. The good
news about Jesus was spread abroad by the apostles and
disciples. They proclaimed first and foremost the death
and resurrection of Jesus the Lord. But they also gave
fuller details about Jesus. They reported what Jesus
taught and the mighty works he performed. Eventually,
after a period of preaching, sometimes referred to as the
"oral tradition", the writers we call evangelists (derived
from the Greek word for gospel, *euaggelion*) recorded the
story of Jesus for future generations. They had understood that the return of the Lord was not imminent, and
took steps to provide reliable accounts of Jesus for the
generations to come. Each gospel contained a record of
the life, death and resurrection of Jesus. Each gospel

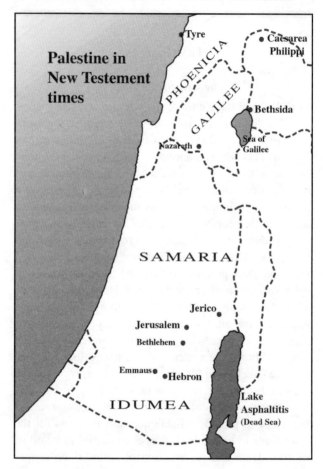

Palestine in New Testement times

Tyre

Caesarea Philippi

PHOENICIA

GALILEE

Bethsida

Nazareth

Sea of Galilee

SAMARIA

Jerico

Jerusalem

Bethlehem

Emmaus

Hebron

Lake Asphaltitis (Dead Sea)

IDUMEA

added to this historical basis the developing understanding about Jesus and his significance.

In all probability it was St Mark who devised the type of writing we know as a gospel. Three of our four gospels are closely related. A comparative study shows without any room for doubt that the evangelists Matthew, Mark and Luke used each other's material. They are called "Synoptics" for they take a similar view. How exactly they related to each other has been the cause of much debate. The vast majority of New Testament scholars now believe that Mark was the first to write a gospel. John's gospel developed quite independently.

The Gospel of Mark

Mark then seems to have invented the gospel genre. It is a presentation of the life of Jesus which explains to the reader the true significance of the person of Jesus and of what he did, so that the reader will be drawn to deeper faith in Jesus. Mark planned his gospel with great skill. Assembling the various pieces of oral tradition, he devised a simple structure for his written gospel. He knew that Jesus had preached in his own region of Galilee, that he had gathered disciples there, preached about the Kingdom of God, and healed the sick. His ministry enjoyed considerable success, though the religious authorities were already concerned about his popularity. Mark knew too that Jesus had not hesitated to make the difficult journey to Jerusalem, the religious and political capital of Palestine. Mark reports one journey of Jesus to Jerusalem. It is the journey to the cross, a journey of acceptance of the cross and of willingness to do the Father's will.

Mark therefore devised a simple but effective structure for the gospel. After initial ministry in Galilee Jesus travels with his disciples on the way to Jerusalem, where, after confrontations with the religious leaders, he is arrested and crucified. The story ends with the discovery that Jesus is alive, raised from the dead. The other synoptic writers, Matthew and Luke, adopted Mark's basic structure and developed it in their different ways.

Before the ministry begins, Mark's gospel has a type of prologue. He declares the faith of Christians in the very first verse of the gospel, proclaiming that Jesus is the Christ, the Messiah (both terms meaning "anointed one"), and that he is the Son of God. Jesus is the anointed one of God, who both fulfilled and challenged the messianic expectations of the time. He is also "Son of God" in a unique sense. Mark continues by reporting John the Baptist's ministry and his baptism of Jesus. At this point the truth about Jesus is proclaimed by the very voice of God: Jesus is the beloved Son, the one with whom the Father is pleased. Jesus is then reported to have gone into the desert to be put to the test by Satan. Jesus is thus the one who comes to confront the evil in the world and to conquer it.

Mark summarises the preaching of Jesus as he begins his ministry in Galilee by showing Jesus proclaim the coming of the kingdom, or the reign, of God. With the coming of God's Son God will re-establish the kingdom. The miracles or mighty works of Jesus illustrate that in Jesus the power of God conquers evil, suffering and death itself. Jesus is the prophet who speaks of the kingdom. His parables illustrate in words what the kingdom is like. His mighty works show the power of the kingdom in deeds.

While the parables of Jesus are less prominent in Mark, the miracles of Jesus take up about one third of Mark's gospel. Some of these are described explicitly as exorcisms, as the expulsion by Jesus of an evil spirit from a person. Some kind of mental sickness may be understood here. In fact, all kinds of sickness and disability, both of mind and of body, were considered in Jesus' day to be the work of Satan. Mark, Matthew and Luke describe Jesus' miracles as "acts of power" or "mighty deeds", by which Jesus overcomes the evil which afflicts the person. It is therefore clear that Jesus proclaims the coming of the kingdom not only in words but also in deeds.

Miracle stories also point to the early Christians' understanding of Jesus and his role. As with all gospel material, the narratives build on the historical traditions to proclaim Christian understanding of Jesus. The story of the stilling of the storm proclaims that Jesus has power over nature. In this he is greater than the prophet Jonah.

While Jonah, according to the Old Testament Book of Jonah, was thrown overboard in order to calm the stormy seas, Jesus brings about calm simply by his powerful word of command. Later in the gospel story, Jesus is the one who reflects the mercy and power of the God of the Exodus, feeding the crowds with bread, and walking on the water. These miracle stories clearly have a strong catechetical dimension.

Jesus gathered disciples around him. Mark portrays them as eager and willing to leave everything and follow him. But Mark also lets us see that they struggle to understand Jesus' teaching. As the journey to Jerusalem begins, the disciples are faced with the difficult issue of the coming suffering of Jesus. He questions the disciples concerning the opinion of the crowds. What expectations does he fulfil? Who is he said to be? Peter declares that Jesus is the Christ, the Messiah. Jesus' response is surprising. He tells Peter that he is to be put to death in Jerusalem and afterwards to be raised. Peter's reaction is one of horror. It is not expected that God's anointed one should suffer martyrdom. Peter tries to dissuade Jesus from risking such a fate and earns the rebuke "Get behind me, Satan!" (Mark 8:33)

The difficulty Peter has is shared by the other disciples. As the journey to Jerusalem continues, Jesus speaks again of his coming death. On each occasion he is met with a puzzled reaction from the disciples. Mark makes clear that the way of being Messiah to which Jesus is called does not match either the expectations of the disciples or those of their contemporaries. This Messiah is to give his life for the world.

Jesus arrives in Jerusalem and symbolically enters the city in humility, riding on an ass. He creates havoc in the Temple as he disrupts the business of those who sell animals for sacrifice and change money into the currency necessary for the Temple tax. The humble Messiah claims back the Temple as a house of prayer for all people. His cursing of the fig tree is a symbol of the judgement deserved by those who do not produce good fruit.

In the final chapters of Mark's gospel the hostility between Jesus and the religious leaders grows. He is to be done away with as a troublesome prophet who has undermined the religious and political peace. As his death approaches Jesus spends the last evening with the chosen disciples. He is keenly aware of the danger he is in. He shares with them a meal which the evangelists describe as a Passover. He gives them the gift of himself with the words over the bread "This is my body" and over the cup "This is my blood, the blood of the covenant, which is poured out for many." *(Mark 14:22-24)* Jesus leaves us his new Passover, the Eucharist.

Mark's presentation of Jesus in Gethsemane shows his anguish as he foresees his torture and execution. The disciples flee when Jesus is arrested. The story of Jesus' death is stark and realistic. Jesus is crucified with two criminals and cries out in desolation: "My God, my God, why have you forsaken me?" *(Mark 15:34)* The words are the opening ones of *Psalm 22*. While Jesus may have recited the whole psalm, the evangelist in quoting its opening words invites us to contemplate the physical and mental agony of Jesus as he experiences the absence of the Father.

It is the centurion who reacts to Jesus' death with words of faith: "This was the Son of God!" *(Mark 15:39)* Mark suggests that it is in seeing Jesus giving his life that believers come to faith. The Son of God gives his life as a ransom for all.

Mark's gospel, like the others, reports the discovery of the empty tomb of Jesus. The empty tomb is explained by a young man in white, who declares the message: "He has been raised. He is not here." *(Mark 16:6)* Although Mark has the young man speak of a meeting in Galilee between the disciples and the risen Lord, the evangelist gives no account of the meeting. The final verses of the canonical gospel *(16:9-20)* are for various reasons considered to be an appendix added later to the gospel. Mark himself seems to end his work with the frightened departure of the women from the empty tomb. Despite the confusion among the disciples, the message of the resurrection of Jesus is clear.

Mark's stress on Jesus' journey to the cross in Jerusalem and his candid portrayal of the struggling disciples, both the twelve who escaped from Gethsemane and the women who fled from the empty tomb, suggest that this is an early gospel possibly written for a Christian community which was experiencing severe persecution and martyrdom. The long-held belief that Mark's gospel was written in Rome by an assistant of St Peter around the time of Nero's persecution remains plausible.

The Gospel of Matthew

Both Matthew and Luke use Mark's gospel, adopting its basic structure, but considerably editing and augmenting it. The three gospels are closely related, but the developing portrayal of Jesus in Matthew and Luke and the vast amounts of new material about Jesus show that these two evangelists have built on Mark's gospel.

A close look at Matthew's gospel will reveal that Matthew adopts Mark's fundamental sequence: a Galilee ministry is followed by a journey to Jerusalem, and the ministry, death and resurrection of Jesus there. Matthew stresses that it is during the Galilee ministry that Jesus proclaims the kingdom. Matthew uses the phrase "kingdom of heaven" rather than "kingdom of God" out of reverence for the name of God. Once the journey to Jerusalem begins Matthew emphasises Jesus' efforts to explain to the disciples that he has to suffer and die.

While Matthew adopts the basic structure of Mark's gospel he also superimposes on this structure five great speeches of Jesus.

Each speech is clearly introduced and ends with a repeated concluding formula, like that at the end of the Sermon on the Mount in Matthew 7:28. The evangelist is able in this way to record substantial amounts of the teaching of Jesus. By assembling the teaching in five discourses he is deliberately alluding to Moses, and the five books of the Law, which are the books of the Pentateuch. Matthew shows that Jesus is the new Moses, and greater than Moses.

Matthew emphasises the point when he reports the words of Jesus: "I have come not to abolish the Law and the Prophets, but to fulfil them." *(Matthew 5:17)* It seems certain that Matthew was writing for a Christian community in which converts from the Jewish faith predominated. The evangelist sets out to show them that fidelity to the God of Moses requires that they welcome Jesus as the new Moses. Matthew inserts into the Gospel a large number of quotations from the Old Testament to illustrate that what happened to Jesus brings the Old Testament to fulfilment.

At the same time, the Gospel of Matthew tends to emphasise the culpability of those Jews who refused to accept Jesus. The gospel record here has been influenced by the antagonism between Christians converted from

Judaism and Jews who did not accept Jesus. At the time of the completion of the Gospel of Matthew the break between Christianity and Judaism had either already taken place or was inevitable. It is important that Christians recognise that this hostility has produced a more negative portrayal of Jesus' contemporaries. The long diatribe of Jesus against the scribes and the Pharisees in chapter 23 seems to be an example of this. Only in Matthew's gospel does the crowd cry out: "His blood be on us and on our children!" *(Matthew 27:25)* Christians should be alert to these negative portrayals of the Jewish people in reading and explaining the Gospel of Matthew.

A more positive picture of Judaism emerges in the Sermon on the Mount in Matthew chapters 5 to 7, for in this most famous of the speeches of Jesus it is apparent how he treasured his Jewish roots. In the Beatitudes, with which the Sermon begins, Jesus adopts a way of speaking found in the Old Testament. Jesus declares that those with specific qualities, such as the poor in spirit, the gentle, the pure in heart, are recipients of God's blessing. But God also blesses those in unavoidable situations of need, those who mourn, the hungry, those who are persecuted. The Sermon continues with the six "antitheses", in which Jesus, having quoted from the current teaching of Judaism, takes the teaching further and deeper with the words "But I say this to you." It is not sufficient to love your neighbour. You are to love your enemy too. Jesus also shows how he treasures the acts of piety in Judaism, almsgiving, prayer and fasting. Jesus teaches the people the Lord's Prayer. He also warns against parading virtuous actions in order to give a good impression.

As Jesus' journey to Jerusalem begins Peter is again seen proclaiming his faith in Jesus only to struggle with the very idea of a suffering Messiah. At this point Matthew includes the commissioning of Peter by Jesus: "You are Peter, and on this rock I will build my Church." *(Matthew 16:18)* The last of the five great speeches of Jesus in chapters 24 to 25 looks to the end of the world and the return of Jesus. Only Matthew gives us the dramatic presentation of the Last Judgement. Service of the least of the brothers and sisters is service of the Lord.

Matthew's story of the death of Jesus is clearly a reworking of Mark with significant additions. Matthew fills in details about the death of Judas. He accentuates the animosity of the crowds clamouring for the death of Jesus. After the discovery of the empty tomb Matthew gives an account of an appearance of Jesus to the disciples in Galilee. A majestic Jesus commissions them to go out to the whole world and preach the gospel to all. The Jesus who came first for his own people sends the disciples out to all the nations.

This brief account of the Gospel of Matthew has not considered the opening chapters of the gospel, which contain the stories of Jesus' birth. We will consider these when we examine the similar material in the Gospel of Luke.

The Gospel of Luke

Like Matthew, Luke also uses the Gospel of Mark. Like Matthew, he adopts Mark's sequence of Galilee ministry, journey to Jerusalem and events in Jerusalem. Like Matthew, Luke edits and augments the gospel. The most significant feature of Luke's restructuring is the lengthening of the section on the journey to Jerusalem from three chapters in Mark to ten chapters in Luke. Luke inserts here further teaching of Jesus, particularly the parables of God's love for sinners and the poor.

Luke's account of Jesus' work in Galilee has a dramatic start. Jesus visits his own town of Nazareth and goes to the synagogue on the sabbath. He reads words from the book of the prophet Isaiah: "The Spirit of the Lord is upon me, for he has anointed me. He has sent me to bring good news to the poor." *(Luke 4:18)* Luke emphasises that this anointed one has come with a particular concern for the poor. The Nazareth visit shows the popularity of Jesus, as he speaks such gracious words. But the story ends with the other dimension of Jesus' ministry. The people become aggressive. The prophet is not accepted by his own people.

The ten chapters of Jesus' journey to Jerusalem contain some of the finest and most treasured pieces of Jesus' teaching in all four gospels. It is in Luke that we find the fullest collection of the parables of Jesus. Jesus used parables to draw comparisons between situations or people familiar to his listeners and the challenge brought by his preaching of the kingdom. Jesus will often use unlikely heroes. When asked about the commandments, Jesus tells the story of the Good Samaritan. His followers are taught to bring help to those in need. He gives as an example a Samaritan, a member of a race despised by the Jews.

Jesus also preaches forgiveness. The parable of the Prodigal Son is one of a set of three in chapter 15. They are directed to the scribes and Pharisees, who are angry at Jesus' association with sinners. The prodigal son comes to his senses and is welcomed back by the father with open arms. The elder brother, like the scribes and Pharisees, is full of resentment. He cannot open his heart to welcome back the one who was lost and is found.

The parable of the Rich Man and Lazarus contains a severe warning to the rich. Despite being consigned to Hades and being unable to reach the bosom of Abraham, the rich man persists in considering Lazarus his inferior. He asks Abraham to send Lazarus to warn his brothers not to follow his example. Even this it seems would not convince them to change their ways.

The parable of the Pharisee and the Tax-Collector points to everyone's need for forgiveness. The tax-collector is presented, like the Samaritan earlier, as a surprising model of conduct for the followers of Jesus. Salvation comes to those who recognise their need of God's forgiveness. It is not earned. The Pharisee by contrast believes he can earn salvation by his good deeds.

Towards the end of the journey, Jesus reaches Jericho. He calls to the chief tax-collector, Zacchaeus, who has climbed a sycamore tree in order to see Jesus. Jesus' visit to his house brings about Zacchaeus' conversion. He will put right any wrong he has done. He too, another tax-collector, becomes a model of conversion and discipleship. Jesus declares that he has come to seek out and save what was lost *(Luke 19:10)*.

The account of Jesus' passion shows significant differences in the Gospel of Luke. Jesus delivers words of encouragement to the disciples at the Last Supper. He praises their fidelity. In Gethsemane Luke makes no mention of their flight. Only Luke shows Jesus tried by both Pilate and Herod the tetrarch. Jesus brings about a reconciliation between them. On the way to Calvary the condemned Jesus considers the plight of the women of Jerusalem. As he is crucified, he forgives the executioners. On the cross he promises salvation to the good thief. Even as he approaches death Luke's Jesus is a bringer of forgiveness and peace. He dies serenely, commending his life to the Father.

Luke gives detailed accounts of the appearances of the risen Jesus. The famous story of the two disciples on their way to Emmaus is found only in Luke. Their gradual recognition of the Lord through his explanation of the Scriptures and then by his breaking of bread proclaims to Christians that Jesus is to be discovered still in the Scriptures and in the Eucharist. The appearance of Jesus to the eleven disciples in Jerusalem stresses the reality of his bodily presence. The Jesus who was crucified and raised from the dead meets the disciples and sends them out to preach the good news. Luke will show the progress of the preaching in the Acts of the Apostles, his second work.

Both Matthew and Luke begin their gospels with two chapters of stories on the birth and infancy of Jesus. The two evangelists both report the essence of the story. Jesus was conceived virginally and born of Mary, who was betrothed to Joseph. The birth took place in Bethlehem during the reign of Herod the Great. Jesus was brought up in Nazareth. Matthew and Luke provide further elaboration of the story in their different ways.

Matthew makes Joseph the focus of attention. He it is who is guided by the angel both to accept Mary as his wife and to protect Mary and the new-born Jesus. Matthew alone tells of the coming of the magi, and of the threat to Jesus' life, which leads to the flight into Egypt. Matthew punctuates the birth stories with quotations from the Old Testament. Luke's chapters are far longer. Luke narrates the conception and birth of both John the Baptist and Jesus. The births are announced to Zechariah, John's father, and to Mary, mother of Jesus. The birth of Jesus is celebrated by angels who communicate good news to the shepherds. While in Matthew it was wise men from foreign lands who worshipped the Messiah, in Luke it is the humble, local shepherds. Luke continues the story with the circumcision of Jesus, the presentation in the Temple in Jerusalem, and a final story of the loss and finding of the boy Jesus when he was twelve years old.

The birth stories provide a further example of how on the basis of the historical tradition each evangelist provides rich reflection on the person and mission of Jesus.

The Gospel of John

John's gospel is quite independent of the synoptic gospels, Matthew, Mark and Luke. It does not follow the sequence provided by Mark. It reports several visits of Jesus to Jerusalem. It lays stronger emphasis on Jesus' identity as the Son of God. But like the three other gospels it uses historical material as the basis for preaching about the person and mission of Jesus.

While Luke's gospel has enjoyed considerable popularity due to Jesus' outreach to the poor and sinners, John's gospel is highly treasured for its depth of doctrine. From the very opening verse we are aware of the profound richness of this evangelist's thought: "In the beginning was the Word." John begins with an extended meditation on the coming of God's Son. He comes as the Word of God, who fully communicates the reality of God. He comes as Light into the darkness of a hostile world. John provides the essence of the doctrine of the incarnation: "The Word became flesh, and lived among us." *(John 1:14)* John is insistent that the Son of God comes as the visible glory of God, to reveal the grace and truth of the Father. While Moses gave the Law, Jesus Christ brings the grace and truth of God. John's Prologue sets the tone for his gospel. It is an extended, meditative exploration of the person of Jesus, the Son of the Father.

John's way of telling the story of the ministry of Jesus begins with the growth to faith of the disciples. As the days of the first week pass, John the Baptist proclaims Jesus as the "Lamb of God", Andrew calls him "Messiah", and the disciples at Cana finally see his glory and believe in him. The miracle at Cana is the first of seven "signs". John calls the miracles "signs" for he is intent on explaining their deeper sense. At Cana Jesus replaces the water for Jewish purification rituals with the wine of the messianic time. The evangelist then narrates two encounters of Jesus in the course of which further clarification of Jesus' mission is provided. To Nicodemus Jesus offers rebirth from above. To the Samaritan woman he promises living water welling up for eternal life.

The later signs of Jesus are often accompanied by extensive discussion between Jesus and the Jews. As in the Gospel of Matthew these detailed dialogues no doubt owe something to the strained relations between Christians and Jews in John's community. When the paralytic is healed on the sabbath in chapter 5, a discussion follows about Jesus' claim that he is always at work, just as his Father is. When he provides bread for the multitudes in chapter 6, there is an extended dialogue in which Jesus presents himself as the bread from heaven who offers believers eternal life. The healing of the man born blind in chapter 9 illustrates Jesus' claim to be the "light of the world". His final sign, the raising of his friend Lazarus from the dead, is preceded by an explanation to both Martha and Mary that he is the resurrection and the life.

In many of these signs Jesus is seen to replace the feasts of Judaism. Just as his wine replaced the water of purification, he is the bread of the new Passover. He offers light and living water to replace these great symbols of the Jewish feast of Tabernacles.

The public ministry of Jesus comes to an end and gives way to a prolonged section set at the Last Supper. The Jesus who has already offered his body and blood to the people as part of the teaching on the bread of life begins the supper by washing the disciples' feet. This symbol of self-giving love accompanies the gift of his body and blood as the final actions of Jesus for his friends before going to his death.

His words at the Last Supper in the Gospel of John fill five chapters. Jesus emphasises his new commandment of love. The disciples are to love each other as Jesus has loved them. When the disciples are confused about his departure Jesus declares: "I am the Way, the Truth and the Life." *(John 14:6)* Jesus is the vine of which the disciples are the branches. He does not leave them alone, but will send the Spirit as an advocate, one who defends and supports them. The Spirit will remind them of Jesus, teaching and leading them forward on the way of truth. *(John 16:13)* John concludes Jesus' words in the upper room with an extended prayer, known as the Priestly Prayer. Jesus intercedes for his disciples and for all those who will come to know him through their preaching. Jesus prays for the unity of all believers.

John's exalted portrayal of Jesus has a marked effect on the story of his passion and death. John underlines the serenity and fortitude of Jesus. This is first apparent in Gethsemane, where the evangelist reports no agony of Jesus, and where the crowds sent to arrest Jesus fall to the ground before him. It is also apparent in the trial of Jesus by Pilate. Pilate is rapidly out of his depth. He does not understand the kingship of Jesus. He has to ask the meaning of the word "truth". But Pilate will unwittingly proclaim to the world the truth about Jesus in his insistence that the title he has had written in three languages should remain fixed to the head of the cross.

Only John reports the presence of the mother of Jesus and the beloved disciple at the foot of the cross. Jesus declares them to be mother and son, a new family of believers. Her faith led to the first of Jesus' signs, at Cana in Galilee. Now she is present again in faithfulness with the disciple at the end. Jesus' final words on the cross are "It is finished." *(John 19:30)* For the evangelist Jesus in dying has completed the work the Father sent him to do.

He dies in triumph. The centurion pierces the side of Jesus, out of which flow blood and water. Jesus in death pours out the waters of new birth. Christians have seen a reference here to Baptism and the Eucharist, the sacraments of new birth. Jesus' burial is fittingly regal. His body is embalmed with an immense quantity of spices.

John's accounts of the risen Jesus are full and graphic. It is Mary Magdalene who is the first to meet the risen Jesus. She is rightly celebrated in the liturgy as the apostle of the resurrection. Jesus bestows the Holy Spirit on the disciples. His appearances to the disciples in Jerusalem culminate in the declaration of full faith by Thomas: "My Lord and my God!" *(John 20:28)*

The final chapter of John's gospel is generally considered to be an appendix, added later to the gospel. The gospel seemed to end with chapter 20 when the evangelist declared that it was written to show the way to faith and life. Chapter 21 narrates an appearance of Jesus by the Sea of Galilee. It is followed by a momentous dialogue between Jesus and Peter. Peter is asked three times if he loves Jesus. This should be understood as an encouragement to Peter to overcome his despondency at denying Jesus. Jesus tells Peter that greater love will be required of him as he grows older. The final words of Jesus are "Follow me!" The gospel record ends in John as it had begun in Mark with the invitation to each individual to become a disciple of Christ.

THE ACTS OF THE APOSTLES

The opening words of the Acts of the Apostles make clear that this is the second work of Luke, addressed as was the first to an important individual named Theophilus. Luke alone takes the story of Jesus further as the good news is preached to the nations. The disciples are told by Jesus to wait for the promised Spirit. The Gospel of John shows Jesus bringing the gift of the Spirit when he appears to the disciples. The Acts of the Apostles contains many accounts of the powerful presence of the Spirit. But it is the account of Pentecost in chapter 2 that most graphically describes the transforming power of the Holy Spirit. According to Luke, crowds had gathered in Jerusalem for the Jewish pilgrimage feast of Pentecost, also called the feast of Weeks. Celebrated on the fiftieth day after Passover, it commemorated the giving of the Law on Mount Sinai. Just as the Law was God's gift to the people of the covenant, so the Spirit is now given to the people of the new covenant and the Church is born.

Peter takes the lead and preaches the first of the great sermons in Acts, sermons which always focus on the death and resurrection of Jesus and present these events as the climax of the history of salvation. Acts reports that three thousand were baptised as a result of Peter's preaching. Luke describes the life of these early Christians and their fidelity to the apostles' teaching, to community living, to the breaking of bread in the Eucharist, and to the prayers.

Acts reports the death of the first martyr, Stephen, and the writer draws parallels between his death and that of Jesus. Both forgive their executioners. Both commend their lives to God. The narrative of Stephen's death gives a brief glimpse of the man who with Peter will play the major role in the rest of Acts. Saul, later to be called Paul, approves of Stephen's killing. The next time Saul appears he will be on the road to Damascus falling prostrate before the Jesus he is persecuting.

A most significant development comes in Acts when Peter is sent to visit the centurion Cornelius. The Spirit comes to Cornelius' household. Peter is convinced that Gentiles too are called to be baptised in the name of Jesus, and he is willing to justify his conduct to his more cautious brethren by speaking of the vision he has seen. Paul meanwhile is even more vigorous in preaching both to Jews and non-Jews. His first missionary journey takes him to Cyprus and Asia Minor (modern Turkey), and his first great discourse, at Antioch in Pisidia, is reported in chapter 13.

The outreach to the pagan Gentiles repeatedly raises the question whether these Christians should be obliged to observe the Jewish Law. Acts chapter 15 narrates a meeting of the leaders in Jerusalem. Under the guidance of the Holy Spirit they decide that the Jewish Law is not to be imposed on those who are not Jews. The significance of this decision can scarcely be overstated. It opened easy access to the Church for pagans, throwing open the gates to people of all nations.

Acts continues with detailed reports of further missionary journeys of St Paul. A most important development comes in chapter 16. Paul receives a vision of a Macedonian asking him to come to his land and help *(Acts 16:9)*. Paul and his companions are convinced that the Spirit is telling them to continue evangelising further west. They cross from Asia to Europe, and head for the Roman colony of Philippi. In both Philippi and Thessalonika Paul experiences persecution from the Jews. When he preaches in Athens he is ridiculed by Gentiles. Acts also reports the founding of the Church at Corinth, and various accounts concerning Paul's time back in Asia Minor at Ephesus. Paul's farewell speech at Miletus in Acts chapter 20 suggests that he too like Jesus is about to journey to the place of martyrdom.

In Jerusalem a riot is incited against Paul for bringing Gentiles to the Temple. It is for his commitment to the mission to non-Jews that hostility against Paul grows. Paul, a Roman citizen, appeals for Roman protection and is taken to Caesarea Marittima, where the successive Roman governors, Felix and Festus, keep him in custody.

Finally Paul is sent to Rome to appeal to the Emperor, suffering a dramatic shipwreck off Malta on the way.

The coming of Paul to Rome brings the focus to the capital of the empire which will become the heart of the universal Church. Why does Acts end with the arrival in Rome and with no reference to the martyrdom of Peter and Paul? Jesus had commanded the disciples to leave Jerusalem and to bring the gospel to the ends of the earth. When they arrived in Rome the two apostles consolidated the Christian faith which had been established there many years earlier. From the capital of the empire the gospel can now be preached to the ends of the earth.

THE LETTERS OF ST PAUL

From our survey of the Acts of the Apostles we know the immense contribution of the apostle Paul to the spread of the Christian faith. But we have a more immediate testimony to his faith and mission in his letters. The genuine letters of St Paul were probably written long before the first gospel was completed. They are thus the earliest writings of the New Testament.

The letters or epistles of St Paul have significant common features. They generally begin with a greeting from Paul and his companions, and end with good wishes and a farewell. Paul's intention in most of them is to strengthen the faith of believers in communities which he himself founded. The Letter to the Romans is an exception to this. It was written to present Paul's teaching to Christians in Rome before he visited them. Paul's intention in his letters is to give advice about the problems the different churches are facing and to develop his teaching about Christ, the Church and the Christian life.

The earliest of Paul's letters is probably the First Letter to the Thessalonians. Paul refers explicitly to his visit to Thessalonika which took place after he and his companions had been badly treated in Philippi, as the Acts of the Apostles testifies. He praises the faith of the Thessalonians and encourages them in their Christian life.

The most significant teaching here concerns the fate of Christians who have died. Paul, who clearly expects the Lord to return in his own lifetime, teaches the Thessalonian Christians that the dead will rise like Jesus. Those still alive at the coming of Christ will have no advantage over those who have died in Christ. Christians furthermore should live in constant expectation of the coming of the Lord. The Second Letter to the Thessalonians sets out to cool any imminent expectations of the return of Christ. Paul taught that Christians should be constantly ready for Christ's coming, and not speculate about the day or the hour.

Paul had founded the Christian community in Corinth, the great commercial city in central Greece. The two letters to the Corinthians which are preserved in the New Testament tell us about the life of the church, its problems and Paul's continuing dealings with the Christians there. It seems that Paul wrote several letters. The second of the two found in the New Testament seems to be composite, containing parts of three separate letters. In the First Letter to the Corinthians Paul provides advice on a great catalogue of issues in the life of the Christians. He speaks of the folly of the cross, of God's foolishness being wiser than human wisdom. He urges unity where factions exist. Problems of sexual morality, legal questions, community worship, the variety of charisms in Christian life, these are among the major themes. In the

final chapters Paul returns to the question of the life of
the resurrection and explains that this life involves a
"spiritual body". There is both continuity and transfor-
mation in Paul's understanding of the risen body. The
Second Letter to the Corinthians contains a vigorous
defence of Paul's status as an apostle, a sign of the sometimes turbulent relationship between Paul and this
church. He also urges local churches to support each
other. Both 2 Corinthians and Acts witness to the fact
that Paul himself made collections in Greece for the poor
of the church in Jerusalem.

Paul writes the Letter to the Philippians from prison.
He encourages the Christians in Philippi to perseverance
and humility. He includes the famous hymn on the self-
abasement and exaltation of Christ (*Philippians 2:5-11*).
For Paul knowledge of Christ is the greatest gift, which
no persecution can take away. He looks forward to shar-
ing in the life of the resurrection. The letter is pervaded
by a deep sense of joy.

The Letter to the Galatians takes up more fully an
issue also found in the Letter to the Philippians.
Christians of Jewish origin are trying to impose obser-
vance of the Law, particularly of the rite of circumcision,
on Christians of pagan origin. It is the issue we noted in
the Acts of the Apostles. Writing to the Galatians Paul
defends his apostolic authority and proclaims his gospel
that salvation comes through faith in Christ and not

through obedience to the Jewish Law. Christians are guided by the Spirit to live in faith and love.

Paul's fundamental preaching of salvation through faith in Christ lies at the heart of his greatest letter, the Letter to the Romans. Paul sends this letter to Rome, which he himself is to visit for the first time on his way to Spain. Christians are justified by faith in Christ. They live in Christ and in his Spirit. Just as sin came into the world through one man, and through sin death, so justification came through the grace of Christ. God's grace, God's justification of sinners, brings unearned forgiveness. Though we are sinners, God treats us as just due to the death of Christ. We receive the undeserved grace of God. We come into this new life by faith in Christ and by Baptism. New life in freedom, guided by the Spirit, replaces the slavery of the old ways of sin and death. Paul then considers the plight of the Jews who have not believed in Christ. God does not withdraw his promises from them. The Jewish people too will be brought to salvation. The letter concludes with the practical implications of the new life in the Spirit. The Letter to the Romans is indeed St Paul's greatest work.

While the Letter to the Romans is the longest of Paul's letters, the Letter to Philemon is the shortest. It deals with a specific pastoral issue, the taking back of a runaway slave. Philemon is a rich Christian whose slave Onesimus has been converted by Paul. Paul intercedes with

Philemon to take Onesimus back, no longer as a slave but as a brother in Christ. While not condemning slavery as such Paul is attacking its fundamental attitudes.

The Letter to the Colossians and the Letter to the Ephesians witness to a development of understanding of Christ and his relationship to the Church. The Letter to the Colossians testifies that strange theories about mysterious heavenly powers are prevalent among them. Paul warns the Colossians against such astrological beliefs. Christ has conquered all such powers by his cross and resurrection. In opposition to Gnostic beliefs that created matter is evil, Paul proclaims Christ as the first-born of all creation, through whom all things were created. He is also the head of the Church, which is his Body, for he is the first to be born from the dead. The Letter to the Ephesians proclaims that Christ brings everything together and ends all division. Gentile and Jew become one in Christ. They form the one Body of Christ, the Church. Paul prays that all Christians will know the love of Christ and be filled with the fulness of God. Both letters go on to give practical moral teaching, particularly about the behaviour of the members of a household.

The two Letters to Timothy and the Letter to Titus have been given the name "pastoral". They provide concrete advice about the care of Christian communities. They are widely considered to have been written by disciples of St Paul. The letters speak of bishops, elders, widows and both male and female deacons. Their required qualities are described. A major emphasis of these letters is that Christians should remain faithful to what they have been taught. The idea of fidelity to the tradition is emerging.

A further letter, traditionally added to the Pauline collection, but considered from earliest times to be written by a different writer, is the Letter to the Hebrews. It is a literary and christological masterpiece. Cleverly constructed to move by stages through complex argumentation, it sets out to explain the nature of the priesthood of Jesus Christ. The Son of God from his place higher than the angels descends to become a brother to men and women. He is described as a trustworthy and compassionate priest, who mirrors and surpasses the priesthood of the Old Testament. This Jesus is described as a priest of the order of Melchizedek, the ancient king who appears in Genesis 14 and Psalm 110. The Messiah has a unique priestly role. He replaces the priests of the Old Testament and renders their worship redundant. He has come to offer himself as the perfect sacrifice, once and for all, by his death on the cross. He thus becomes the source of salvation for all and opens access to God's heavenly temple. He inaugurates a new covenant for believers. The Letter is a masterly demonstration of the fulfilment of the Old Testament in the New. Christians are encouraged on their journey of faith, hope and love.

THE OTHER LETTERS

The seven letters outside the Pauline collection have been known since the early centuries as the "Catholic Epistles", for they are not directed to specific local churches. The focus in their titles is on the traditional writers, not on those to whom they are addressed. Letters are attributed to James and Jude, two letters to Peter, and three to John.

Though the Letter of James begins like a letter it does not end like one. It is a collection of wise teachings for believers in Jesus. Trials should be considered as privileges. True religion means assisting those in need and remaining unstained by the world. Faith is to be lived out in good works. The sick are to be anointed by the elders of the Church. It is a rich compendium of moral teaching. The writer describes himself as a servant of God and of the Lord Jesus (*James 1:1*). Tradition equates him not with either of the apostles called James, but with James "the brother of the Lord", who became the leader of the Jerusalem church and is mentioned by St Paul and in the Acts of the Apostles.

The First Letter of Peter begins as a letter addressed to Christians in various parts of Asia Minor. After the initial greeting the writer praises God's gift of new birth in Christ. Despite hardship Christians remain faithful, rejoicing in their new life in Christ. Baptism makes Christians a royal priesthood. They are living stones in the spiritual house of which Christ is the foundation. The writer then spells out some practical challenges of Christian faith. He has particularly encouraging words for the elders. They are to shepherd the flock and watch over it on behalf of Christ, the chief shepherd. They are to do so with no thought for personal gain.

The Second Letter of Peter reproduces most of the Letter of Jude, which raises doubts about authorship by St Peter. The author of the Letter of Jude is described as "Jude, servant of Jesus Christ and brother of James" (*Jude v.1*). The letter denounces false teachers who would undermine faith in Jesus Christ, and replace grace with licentiousness. The Second Letter of Peter, as well as adopting and repeating most of the Letter of Jude, also gives encouragement to live the Christian life to the full. It speaks of the inadequacy of individual interpretation of Scripture, and urges Christians to wait in patience for the new heavens and the new earth.

As we would expect, the three Letters of John have significant links with the Gospel of John. In style and vocabulary there are so many similarities. A major difference is that the struggle in the gospel against the Jews is replaced by a struggle against Christians who are deserting the community. These people have undermined the message of the incarnation and deny the importance of the human life of the Son of God. His divinity and their share in it is enough. They seem to believe that salvation came from the entry into the world of the Son of God, not from his death on the cross. They consider that once they have become children of God by faith their human activities are likewise unimportant. For the writer of the letter the true child of God, saved by the death of Christ, must avoid sin, and keep the commandments. As in the Gospel of John it is the commandment of love given by Jesus which should be the principal concern.

The Second and Third Letters of John are brief. The Second Letter encourages an unnamed local church to continue on the ways of love. They are warned not to welcome those who have deserted the true teaching. The Third Letter is addressed to a certain Gaius to commend and encourage the hospitality he has shown to preachers of the truth.

THE BOOK OF REVELATION

The final book of the New Testament, the Apocalypse of
John, or the Book of Revelation, presents considerable
problems of interpretation. It has been misinterpreted constantly. To read it correctly, it is particularly important to
be aware of the type of writing it represents. The reader
must take note of what scholars call the "literary genre".
Just as a gospel can be misinterpreted if the reader fails to
acknowledge that the gospel genre is both historical and
catechetical, similarly here there will be misunderstanding
if the reader does not appreciate the basic qualities of what
is called "apocalyptic writing".

This type of writing, popular among the Jews from the
second century BC and then also among Christians, presents the visions of a visionary or seer, usually a well-
known authoritative figure, concerning the liberation from
present crisis and the establishment of the reign of God in
the coming last days. The visions are expressed in code,
for they are written in time of persecution. Our New
Testament Book of Revelation is no exception. It has an
obvious background in the persecution of the church by
the Roman empire. All twenty-two chapters of the book
are presented in a vision, even the seven letters to the
churches of Asia Minor in the opening chapters. A revelation given by God to Jesus is entrusted to a man named

John. John has written down this revelation, or apocalypse. It is uncertain who this John was, though tradition
has linked him with the evangelist of the same name.

What makes the visions in the Book of Revelation difficult is their constant use of imagery and of quotations
from the Old Testament. Once the images, such as that of
Christ as the Lamb, and that of the Roman empire as the
beast, are deciphered, interpretation is made easier. Once
the relevance of the Old Testament quotations, often from
the Book of Daniel, is appreciated, a rich understanding is
opened up. This is not easy material to fathom.

In his visions we are brought with the visionary to the
throne of God in heaven. Twenty-four elders and four animals surround God's throne. The elders, representing the
tribes of Israel and the apostles of the Church, praise God as
creator. The animals, perhaps intended as cherubs, glorify
God. The focus is then on the scroll with seven seals which
is in the right hand of God. For history to be brought to its
end someone must take the scroll and open the seals. It is
the Lamb that was slain that is able to do this. The Son of
God, who died and was raised, is able under the Father's
gaze to bring the events of history to a close.

As the visions continue the focus is ever more concen-
trated on both the trials and triumphs of God's people in
the last times. The victory of God over the forces of evil
is assured. The final vision in the book describes the new
Jerusalem, the new city of God, where God dwells for

ever with the people. A rich collection of Old Testament scripture is used to describe the triumph of God and of the saints. God will wipe away every tear. Everything will be made new. The water of life will be provided. In the new Jerusalem people will see God face to face. It will never be night again. No lamplight or sunlight will be necessary. The Lord God will be the light of all.

It should not surprise us that the New Testament, and the whole Bible, ends in visions, for their imagery suggests that we are to see things no human eye has ever seen. God speaks to human minds through the language of imagination to provide some grasp of the good things God has prepared for us. The Book of Revelation proclaims the hope of Christians that through the work of Christ, the Lamb who was slain and now lives for ever, the way is open to life with God. The book ends with the prayer of Christians, "Maranatha", "Come, Lord." It is the prayer inspired by the reading of this book. It is the prayer inspired by the Spirit in the hearts of Christians as they read and contemplate the writings of the New Testament.

Further Reading on the New Testament

THE DOGMATIC CONSTITUTION ON DIVINE REVELATION
(Second Vatican Council) *Dei Verbum* (Do 361)

THE INTERPRETATION OF THE BIBLE IN THE CHURCH,
(Pontifical Biblical Commission) Pauline Books and Media

R.E. Brown, *Responses to 101 Questions on the Bible*, London,
Geoffrey Chapman, 1991

R.E. Brown, *An Introduction to the New Testament*, New York,
Doubleday, 1997

A. Graffy, *Trustworthy and True. The Gospels Beyond 2000*, Dublin,
Columba Press, 2001

D. Harrington, *Revelation. The Book of the Risen Christ (Spiritual Commentaries)*, Hyde Park NY, New City Press, 1999

J. P. Meier, *A Marginal Jew. Rethinking the Historical Jesus*, (volume 1), New York, Doubleday, 1991

J. Murphy-O'Connor, *Paul. A Critical Life*, Oxford, Clarendon Press, 1996

Appendix: Dei Verbum on the Formation of the Gospels

(and Catechism of the Catholic Church paragraphs 124-127.)

n.18 It is common knowledge that among all the inspired writings, even among those of the New Testament, the Gospels have a special place, and rightly so, because they are our principal source for the life and teaching of the Incarnate Word, our Saviour.

The Church has always and everywhere maintained, and continues to maintain, the apostolic origin of the four Gospels. The apostles preached, as Christ had charged them to do, and then, under the inspiration of the Holy Spirit, they and others of the apostolic age handed on to us in writing the same message they had preached, the foundation of our faith: the fourfold Gospel, according to Matthew, Mark, Luke and John.

n.19 Holy Mother Church has firmly and with absolute constancy maintained and continues to maintain, that the four Gospels just named, whose historicity she unhesitatingly affirms, faithfully hand on what Jesus, the Son of God, while he lived among men, really did and taught for their eternal salvation, until the day when he was taken up (*cf. Acts 1:1-2*). For, after the ascension of the Lord, the apostles handed on to their hearers what he had said and done, but with that fuller understanding which they, instructed by the glorious events of Christ and enlightened by the Spirit of truth, now enjoyed. The sacred authors, in writing the four Gospels, selected certain of the many elements which had been handed on, either orally or already in written form, others they synthesized or explained with an eye to the situation of the churches, the while sustaining the form of preaching, but always in such a fashion that they have told us the honest truth about Jesus. Whether they relied on their own memory and recollections or on the testimony of those who "from the beginning were eyewitnesses and ministers of the Word," their purpose in writing was that we might know the "truth" concerning the things of which we have been informed (*cf. Lk. 1:2-4*).

From the Catechism of the Catholic Church

124 "The Word of God, which is the power of God for salvation to everyone who has faith, is set forth and displays its power in a most wonderful way in the writings of the New Testament" which hand on the ultimate truth of God's Revelation. Their central object is Jesus Christ, God's incarnate Son: his acts, teachings, Passion and glorification, and his Church's beginnings under the Spirit's guidance.

125 The Gospels are the heart of all the Scriptures "because they are our principal source for the life and teaching of the Incarnate Word, our Saviour".

126 We can distinguish three stages in the formation of the Gospels:

    1. The life and teaching of Jesus. The Church holds firmly that the four Gospels, "whose historicity she unhesitatingly affirms, faithfully hand on what Jesus, the Son of God, while he lived among men, really did and taught for their eternal salvation, until the day when he was taken up."

    2. The oral tradition. "For, after the ascension of the Lord, the apostles handed on to their hearers what he had said and done, but with that fuller understanding which they, instructed by the glorious events of Christ and enlightened by the Spirit of truth, now enjoyed."

    3. The written Gospels. "The sacred authors, in writing the four Gospels, selected certain of the many elements which had been handed on, either orally or already in written form; others they synthesized or explained with an eye to the situation of the churches, the while sustaining the form of preaching, but always in such a fashion that they have told us the honest truth about Jesus."

127 The fourfold Gospel holds a unique place in the Church, as is evident both in the veneration which the liturgy accords it and in the surpassing attraction it has exercised on the saints at all times:

There is no doctrine which could be better, more precious and more splendid than the text of the Gospel. Behold and retain what our Lord and Master, Christ, has taught by his words and accomplished by his deeds.

But above all it's the gospels that occupy my mind when I'm at prayer; my poor soul has so many needs, and yet this is the one thing needful. I'm always finding fresh lights there; hidden meanings which had meant nothing to me hitherto.

The unity of the Old and New Testaments

128 The Church, as early as apostolic times, and then constantly in her Tradition, has illuminated the unity of the divine plan in the two Testaments through typology, which discerns in God's works of the Old Covenant prefigurations of what he accomplished in the fullness of time in the person of his incarnate Son.

129 Christians therefore read the Old Testament in the light of Christ crucified and risen. Such typological reading discloses the inexhaustible content of the Old Testament; but it must not make us forget that the Old Testament retains its own intrinsic value as Revelation reaffirmed by our Lord himself. Besides, the New Testament has to be read in the light of the Old. Early Christian catechesis made constant use of the Old Testament. As an old saying put it, the New Testament lies hidden in the Old and the Old Testament is unveiled in the New.

130 Typology indicates the dynamic movement toward the fulfillment of the divine plan when "God [will] be everything to everyone." Nor do the calling of the patriarchs and the exodus from Egypt, for example, lose their own value in God's plan, from the mere fact that they were intermediate stages.

CTS
MEMBERSHIP

We hope you have enjoyed reading this booklet. If you would like to read more of our booklets or find out more about CTS - why not do one of the following?

1. Join our Readers CLUB.
We will send you a copy of every new booklet we publish, through the post to your address. You'll get 20% off the price too.

2. Support our work and Mission.
Become a CTS Member. Every penny you give will help spread the faith throughout the world. What's more, you'll be entitled to special offers exclusive to CTS Members.

3. Ask for our Information Pack.
Become part of the CTS Parish Network by selling CTS publications in your own parish.

Call us now on 020 7640 0042 or return this form to us at CTS, 40-46 Harleyford Road, London SE11 5AY
Fax: 020 7640 0046 email: info@cts-online.org.uk

❏ I would like to join the *CTS Readers Club*

❏ Please send me details of how to join CTS as a *Member*

❏ Please send me a *CTS Information Pack*

Name:...

Address: ....

....

Post Code:..

Phone: ....

email address: ....

Registered charity no. 218951.
Registered in England as a company limited by guarantee no.57374.

Text acknowledgments

Quotations from the *Confession* and the *Letter to Coroticus* are taken
from *The Confession of St Patrick*, translated by John Skinner, an
Image book published by Doubleday, c/o Bantam Doubleday Dell
Publishing Group Inc., 1540 Broadway, New York, NY 10036.
Quotations from the 'Deer's Cry' (*Faeth Fiada*) are taken from
John Skinner's translation published in the same volume, excluding
extract 12, which is translated by Whitley Stokes and taken from
Celtic Christianity: Ecology and Holiness by William Parker Marsh and
Christopher Bamford, published by Floris Books, 15 Harrison
Gardens, Edinburgh EH11 1SH.

Picture acknowledgments

Cover (landscape): Jean Williamson/Mick Sharp;
2–3, 9, 16–17, 23, 28–29, 36–37, 42–43: Images Colour Library;
10, 19, 27, 39, 40: Nicholas Rous; 33: Mick Sharp;
46: Bord Fáilte – Irish Tourist Board

All artwork by Vanessa Card

THE TRUE SUN

For this sun which we now see
Rises each new day for us at his command,
Yet it will never reign,
Nor will its splendour last for ever.
But we who believe and adore
The true sun that is Christ
Will never die, nor will those
Who have done his will,
But will abide for ever,
Just as Christ himself will abide
for all eternity,
Who reigns with God the Father all-powerful,
And with the Holy Spirit before time began,
And now and through all ages of ages.

Amen.

Confession, V:60